## Farshore

First published in Great Britain 2021 by Farshore
An imprint of HarperCollins*Publishers,*
1 London Bridge Street, London SE1 9GF
www.farshore.co.uk

HarperCollins*Publishers,* 1st Floor, Watermarque Building, Ringsend Road Dublin 4, Ireland

Written by Laura Jackson. Designed by Jeannette O'Toole

© 2021 Disney Enterprises, Inc.
The movie THE PRINCESS AND THE FROG copyright © 2009, Disney, inspired in part by the book
THE FROG PRINCE by E. D. Baker copyright © 2002, published by Bloomsbury Publishing, Inc.

ISBN 978 0 7555 0101 4
Printed in Italy
001

A CIP catalogue record for this title is available from the British Library.

This *Disney Princess*
2022 Annual belongs to

.......................................................

.......................................................

# Disney
# PRINCESS
## Annual 2022

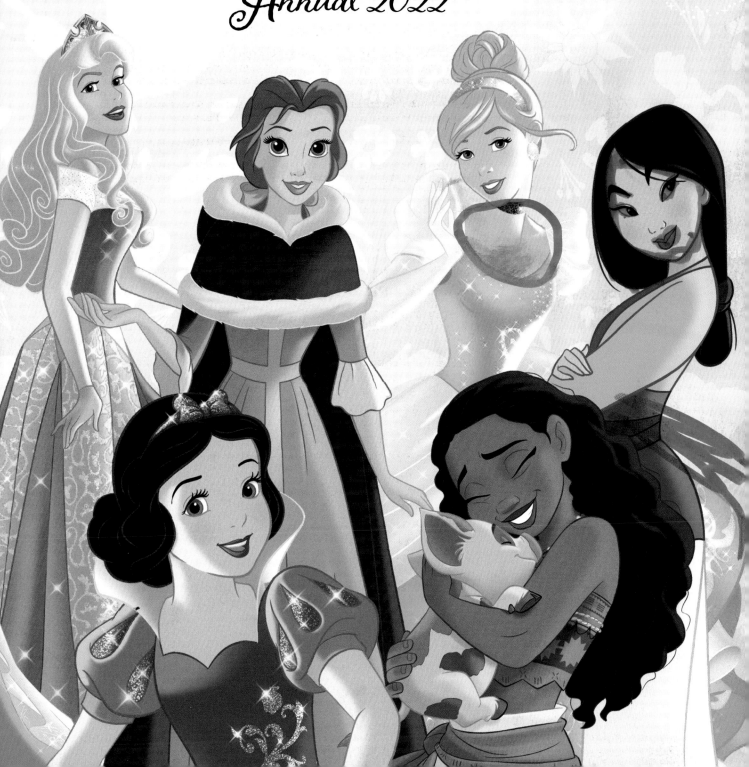

# Contents

# Meet ... Cinderella

* **Cinderella is ...** ~~stupid~~ caring, loving and hard-working.

* **Cinderella loves ...** ~~POOP~~ her pet dog, Gus!

* **Cinderella believes ...** ~~nothing~~ you should never give up.

* **Cinderella's story ...** ~~isss~~ When Cinderella's father dies, her stepmother is mean to Cinderella. She makes her scrub the house every day, but Cinderella never stops dreaming. When an invitation to the Royal Ball arrives, her Fairy Godmother tranforms Cinderella into a princess and her life changes forever.

# Royal Maze

Prince Charming is looking everywhere for Cinderella.
Guide him through the maze to her.

Make sure
you collect
the glass slipper
along the way!

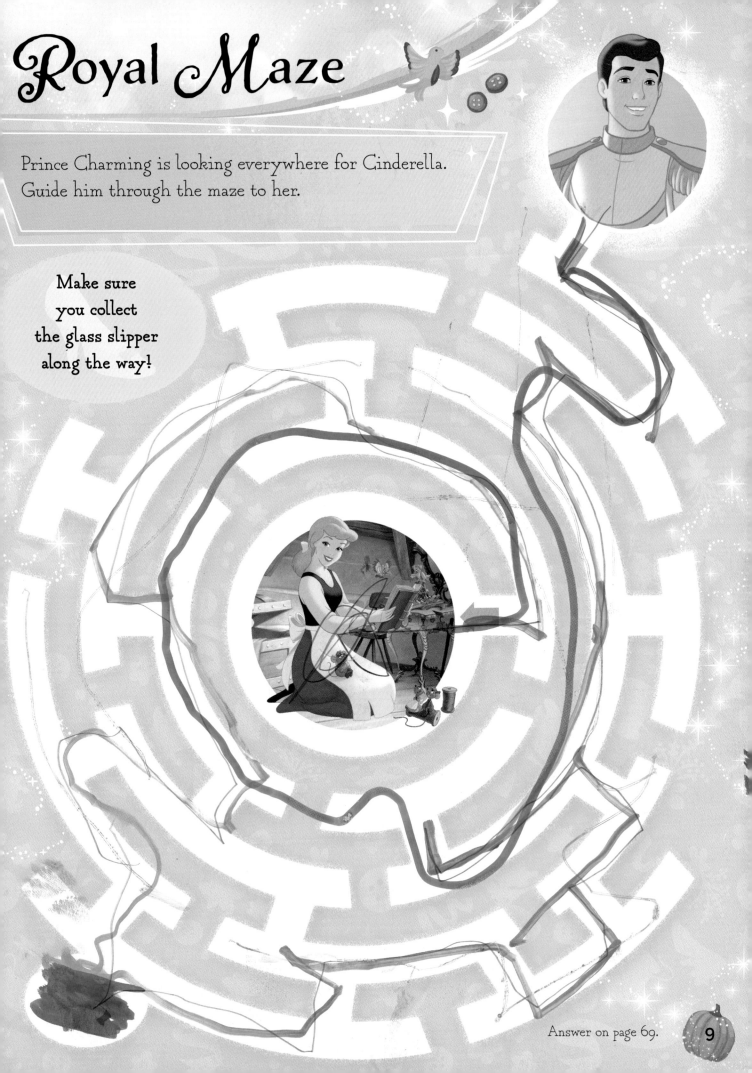

Answer on page 69.

# A New Friend

**1** One morning, Jaq and Gus excitedly beckoned Cinderella to follow them to the palace garden. It was clear that something was wrong ...

**2** ... but it was hard for Cinderella to guess what her two friends were telling her.

**3** After much guessing, the mice suddenly jumped up and ran off. "A pear thief?" Cinderella thought as she rushed after her friends.

**1** Follow the mice to the thief.

**4** There in the palace garden, a beautiful chestnut colt pulled at a branch on the pear tree. The little horse shook the branch to pull off a pear.

**5** "Why you sillies, it's not a thief," said Cinderella, "it's just a beautiful but very hungry colt."

**6** Just then, the colt dashed off with a pear in his mouth. Cinderella followed the colt into the forest.

**7** Cinderella could not keep up with the speedy colt. But she followed the direction the colt ran and soon she discovered him together with another horse, a beautiful chestnut mare!

**2** Circle the fruit the colt has in his mouth.

Answer on page 69.

**8** The colt nuzzled up against the mare who had her leg stuck in a log. "This must be your mother," said Cinderella. "How sweet of you to bring her the pear."

**10** The mare was very happy when she could finally stand up again. "Let's get you to the palace stables for a proper meal and some water," said Cinderella.

**9** "Now hold very still," said Cinderella as she began to free the mare's leg. It was hard but she managed.

**3** Tick ✔ what Cinderella will give the two horses.

**a** Food and water ✔

**b** New shoes ✔

Answer on page 69.

**11** And now that the colt was no longer a dangerous thief Gus and Jaq introduced themselves. The colt looked at them curiously.

**12** Then the colt lowered his head in front of them. Gus and Jaq looked up at Cinderella "Go on boys," urged Cinderella. "He's offering you a ride."

**13** The two mice smiled shyly and then climbed up onto the little colt. Jaq and Gus were the first riders that the colt had ever had and he galloped along happily.

**4** Colour the flowers when you finish.

**14** The chestnut mare looked at her lovely colt, her heart full of pride. Her little colt and its two small friends had bravely saved the day!

*The End*

# Perfect Pet

Cinderella loves playing with her pet dog, Bruno. He gives the best cuddles!

Spot 6 differences between the pictures. Circle a mouse every time you find a difference.

Answers on page 69.

# A Magic Spell

Help the Fairy Godmother to magic up a new dress for Cinderella.

**1** Point to the glass slipper.

**2** Draw over the dotty magic wand trail.

**3** Trace over the dots to make Cinderella's dress appear. Now colour it in.

# Meet ... Tiana

**❊ Tiana is ...**
determined, talented and clever.

**✳ Tiana loves ...**
cooking delicious food.

**❀ Tiana believes ...**
in following your dreams.

**❊ Tiana's story ...**
Tiana dreams of opening her own restaurant. She saves every penny and works hard every day to make her dreams come true. It's only when she accidentally turns into a frog and meets Prince Naveen, that she realises that love is just as important as hard work!

*The only way to get what you want is through hard work!*

# Talented Tiana

Tiana cooks delicious food for the people in her restaurant. Help her gather the vegetables needed for her yummy soup. Collect them in the order shown to lead you to the bowl.

# Memory Game

Tiana has a list of things she needs to buy for her restaurant. Can you help her remember everything?

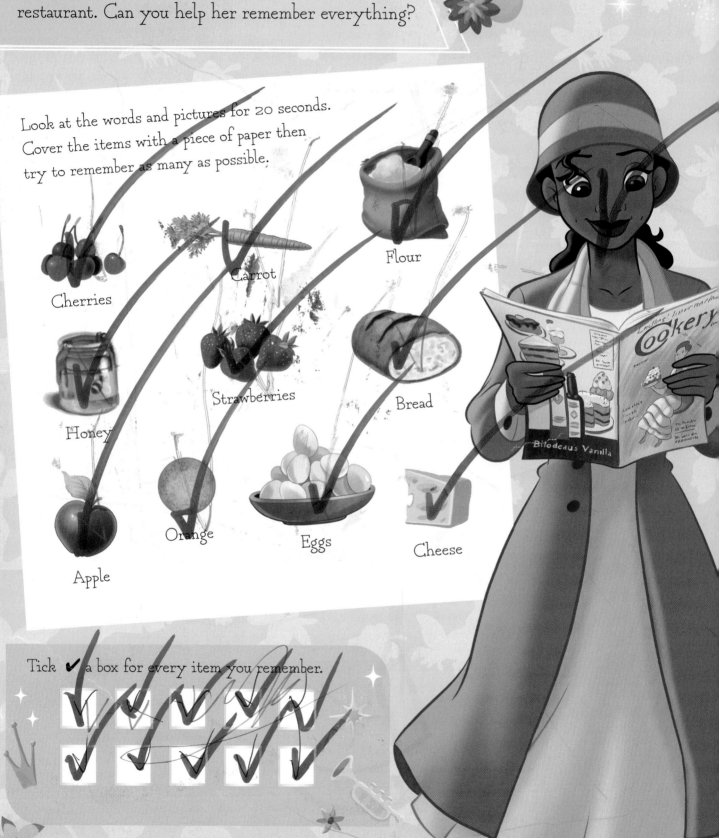

Look at the words and pictures for 20 seconds. Cover the items with a piece of paper then try to remember as many as possible.

Cherries

Carrot

Flour

Honey

Strawberries

Bread

Apple

Orange

Eggs

Cheese

Tick ✔ a box for every item you remember.

# Dream Big

Tiana's big dream was to open her own restaurant. She worked hard to make that dream come true. Draw some pictures of your big dreams.

You could draw **your dream job,** **your dream holiday** or **your dream house.**

Satt

Cafe
The
Place

The Weigh
inn
OK

Poo

*Now you just have to make your dreams come true!*

# Meet ...

## Belle

- **Belle is** ~~poop~~ true, loyal and not afraid to be different.

- **Belle loves** ~~her private~~ reading and learning new things.

- **Belle believes** ~~nothing~~ in seeing the best in people.

- **Belle's story** ~~about poop~~ Belle has always dreamed of a life outside her little town. When she visits the Beast in his castle, she soon finds the good in him that nobody else can see. While everybody in her town is afraid of the Beast, Belle risks everything to save his life.

~~Don~~ *Be beautiful inside and out.*

# Book of Dreams

Belle loves to read stories. Can you design
your very own book for Belle to read?
Remember to give it a title!

# Furry Intruder

**1** One morning, Belle poured herself a glass of milk. She briefly turned away to get some cookies out of the oven, but when she turned back, the glass was empty. Who had drunk her milk?

*How strange!*

*It wasn't me. I drink tea!*

Who do you think drank the milk?

**2** Later, Mrs. Potts told the other enchanted objects about the strange story of the empty milk glass. "Perhaps it was the Beast who drank it?" suggested Chip. "But he was in the garden all morning," insisted Lumière.

**3** "Then who could it be?" asked Chip. "I think I know who!" said Cogsworth. "Come, I will show you."

**4** Cogsworth led the enchanted objects to a broken vase in the dining room. "I was taking a short nap," he began, "but was awakened by a big CRASH! Someone broke the vase!"

*Oh my!*

*Who did it?*

**1** Can you count how many pieces the vase broke into?

**6** "My poor Fifi," said Lumière. "I think it is clear that we have an intruder in the castle and we must get it out!"

*He's right!*

**5** Next, Fifi spoke up. "I too heard a most horrible sound. Someone was scratching at the door while I dusted the library!"

*We'll get him!*

**7** They all agreed not to tell Belle. So that night, the enchanted objects patrolled the castle, watching for the intruder.

**8** "We'll catch that milk-drinking, vase-breaking, door-scratching monster and throw him out!" declared Cogsworth, as he marched back and forth in the hall.

**9** Everyone patrolled their stations until late at night. But the intruder didn't appear. When the clock struck midnight, they were all very tired.

**10** They agreed it was best to patrol together in the hall. "I think I will just take a quick nap," said Lumière. "Wake me up if you hear the intruder." They all nodded but fell asleep too!

ZZZZZZZ

**11** The next morning, Belle found everyone lying asleep in the hall. "What is going on here?" asked Belle.

**2** Circle the things they carried on patrol.

a    b    c    d    e    f    g    h    i

**12** *"Madame, we were trying to catch the intruder!" answered Lumière. "What intruder?" asked Belle. "The one who drank our milk!" said Cogsworth.*

*You're not a monster at all!*

*What a sweet kitty!*

**13** *Belle giggled, "I think I've found your intruder. This stable kitten must have got stuck inside the castle. I found her curled up in my bed this morning!" It was the kitten that had drunk Belle's milk, broken the vase and scratched at the door. When they took the kitten back to the stables they all agreed it was the furriest and cutest intruder they had ever seen.*

*The End*

**3**

Circle the five things that are different in this picture.

Answers on page 69.

# Adventurous Belle

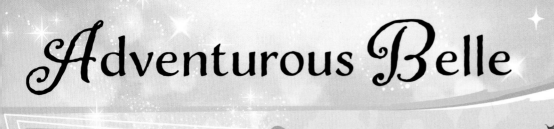

Belle loves racing around on the ice rink.

**1**

Finish colouring Belle's cape.

**2**

Use your pencil to trace over Belle's skating words.

jump

slippery

hard

frosty

fun fast ice

Can you think of any other words that describe ice skating?

Trace over each trail and do the action when you get to the end.

Tippy-toe up and down 5 times.

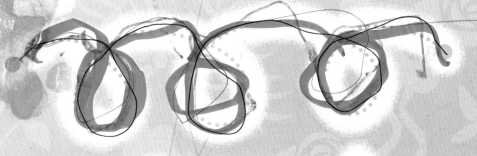

Twirl around 3 times.

Jump up high, arms stretched upwards 2 times.

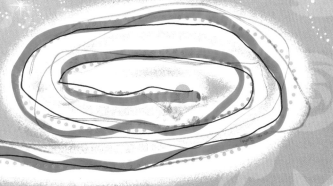

Curl up into a small ball.

Pretend you are walking a tightrope. Put one foot in front of the other and walk across the room.

# Meet ... Moana

 **Moana is ...**
daring, spirited and brave.

**Moana loves ...**
the ocean, her family and her pet pig, Pua!

**Moana dreams ...**
of having big ocean adventures.

**Moana's story ...**
Ever since Moana was a baby, she could feel the call of the ocean. Her father does everything to keep Moana on the land but when her island is in danger, Moana sets sail. She bravely journeys across the ocean on a daring quest to save the people of Motunui!

*The ocean chose me!*

# Ocean Adventure

Young Moana loves the ocean so much she even goes surfing with her pet pig, Pua!

*This picture was coloured by*

me Scott Johnston

that did amazing

# Coconut Fun

Moana, Pua and the village rooster, Heihei, are harvesting coconuts.

**1** Tick ✔ the smallest coconut.

a    b    c

**2** Circle the biggest coconut.

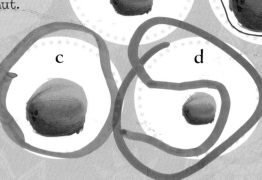

a    b    c    d

**3** Find the 2 halves that look exactly the same.

 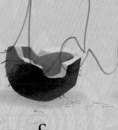 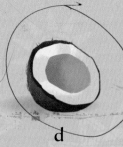

a    b    c    d

Answer on page 69.

# Moana the Hero

Moana needs to get to Te Fiti to save the island of Motunui. Can you help her find a route through the waves? Count how many floating flowers Moana passes along the way.

I counted 4 flowers.

START

FINISH

Answer on page 69.

# Pua Saves the Day

That looks right for a chief!

**1** The feast to welcome spring was starting soon and Moana wanted to make an anklet for her father as a surprise gift. After a lot of searching, she found the perfect shell for the anklet.

**1** Circle what Heihei is pecking in the picture.

a   b   c

**2** The villagers were all preparing food for the feast but Heihei was getting in everyone's way. Gramma Tala sighed as the silly bird got his foot caught in a woven platter.

**3** Gramma Tala freed Heihei but slipped on the platter. As Moana caught her, the anklet she'd been hiding in her belt fell and landed around Heihei's neck. Nobody noticed.

**4** Gramma Tala decided to put Heihei in a basket until after the feast so he couldn't cause any more trouble. She still didn't spot the anklet around his neck.

**5** Just then, Moana realised the anklet was missing. Her pet pig Pua peered inside the basket and spotted it around Heihei's neck. He was determined to get the anklet back for Moana.

**6** But first, Pua needed to get the basket open. He tried rolling it, catapulting it and dragging it. Heihei's head and feet popped out but the strong basket stayed shut.

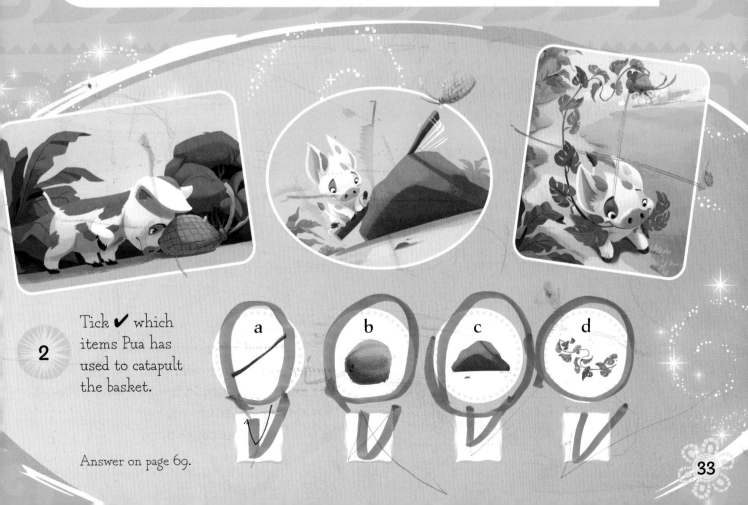

**2** Tick ✔ which items Pua has used to catapult the basket.

a ✔    b ✗    c ✗    d ✔

Answer on page 69.

**8** Pua bounced up and down on a branch and the two animals were flung out of the tree. They soared through the air towards the feast. As the basket hit the ground, it finally opened.

**7** Then Pua heard music - the feast was about to start. He had to do something drastic to get the anklet to Moana in time. He tossed the basket into a tree and jumped up after it ...

**9** Pua and Heihei rolled across the beach, getting tangled up in a fishing net, and came to a stop right by Moana's feet. "You found it!" she cried, taking the anklet from Pua's snout.

**3** Follow the trail Pua and Heihei have made, soaring through the sky.

**10** *Later that evening, Moana gave her father the anklet. "I love it," he said, giving her a hug. Moana smiled gratefully at Pua to say thank you to her loyal pet for saving the day.*

*I'll treasure it forever.*

**11** *Then she rolled her eyes as Heihei wandered past, tangled up in the basket again with a piece of driftwood stuck on his beak. Some things never change!*

**The End**

**4** Draw an anklet for Moana to wear.

# Meet ... *Ariel*

⭐ **Ariel is ...**
curious, adventurous and trusting.

🐚 **Ariel loves ...**
singing, collecting treasures and exploring.

🐚 **Ariel wishes ...**
to be part of the human world.

✴ **Ariel's story ...**
Ariel's father will not allow her to go to the surface, but rules don't stop Ariel. She soon finds herself rescuing a human prince! When a wicked sea witch called Ursula takes Ariel's voice, Ariel is put in great danger. Luckily, love will always save the day!

*Isn't it fantastic?*

# Under the Sea

Ariel's life underwater is full of friends, family and fun.

**1** Colour the seashell underneath the odd picture out in each row.

## ROW 1

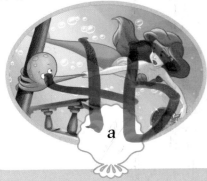
a

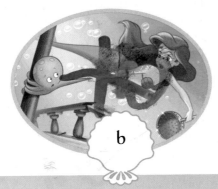
b

c

## ROW 2

a

b

c

## ROW 3

a

b

c

**2** Cross out the things that don't belong in the sea.

Answer on page 69.

# Ocean Doodles

Wow! Ariel and Flounder have discovered treasure at the bottom of the ocean. The fish want to look, too.

**1** Draw lots of fish. Give each one a different pattern.

**2** Tick ✔ a box every time you see a shell.

**3** Colour in Flounder.

Answer on page 69.

38

Join the dots
on Ariel's tail
and then colour
it green.

# Wishing Shell

**1** *Ariel was busy trying to retrieve a seashell from the seabed which had caught her eye. The pretty shell glowed as if it were magic.*

**What's this?**

**2** *"What a beautiful shell," Ariel said. She imagined what it would be like to have a magical shell that could grant wishes.*

**1**

Tick ✔ what Ariel has found.

**3** *First, she dreamt that she was riding a seahorse in a competition and she won first prize.*

4     Then she dreamt she was the star of a singing contest surrounded by a school of fish who performed a dazzling dance routine.

*If only it could grant wishes.*

5     Suddenly, Sebastian appeared and snapped her out of her daydream. Ariel told him she was disappointed that the shell wasn't really magical and able to make her dreams come true.

6     "Dreams are important but only if we achieve them by our own hard work," said Sebastian.

*Ocean Contest*

7     Ariel decided she was going to make her dreams come true herself. She was going to organise an ocean contest and everyone was invited to show off their talents and skills.

**8** First, she asked her friends to help with the poster and invitations. Then she asked King Triton if he would judge the contest.

**2** Write who made the poster.

Sebastian

**9** Next, Ariel organised the seahorses for the race competition. Then she assembled the band and sorted out rehearsals for the singing and dance competitions. She even made pretty sea-garlands to give out as prizes.

*All done!*

*I know.*

**10** "What are you going to give as first prize to the overall winner?" asked Flounder. "Oh dear, I hadn't thought of that. I wish..."

**3** Colour the sea flowers.

11 Suddenly, Ariel had an idea. "I'll give the overall winner this beautiful shell!" she said excitedly. "It's a perfect prize," agreed Flounder.

12 The day of the contest arrived. Ariel was happy that all her hard work had paid off. Everyone enjoyed the contest and lots of prizes were given out. But there could only be one overall winner.

13 After a long pause, King Triton made his announcement, "The first prize is for... 'Best Ocean Contest Organiser' and the winner is Ariel!" Everyone cheered as Ariel received her well-deserved prize.

# Meet ...
# Mulan

**Mulan is ...**
clever, loyal and a fearless leader.

**Mulan loves ...**
her family, her pets and winning battles!

**Mulan hopes ...**
to always make her family proud.

**Mulan's story ...**
When Mulan's sick father is called up to fight with the Imperial Army, Mulan disguises herself as a man to take his place. She bravely uses her skills to battle against the enemy and brings honour to her family.

*Be your own hero!*

# Fearless Mulan

Mulan bravely takes the place of her father in a battle despite all the dangers.

**1**

Colour the flower below the odd one out in each row.

**2**

Follow the line to find Mulan's 'lucky' friend. Do you know his name?

**ROW 1**

a

b

c

**ROW 2**

a

b

c

**ROW 3**

a

b

c

Answer on page 69.

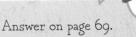

# Time for Courage

Once upon a time there was a clever Chinese girl named Mulan. She disguised herself as a man to take her sickly father's place in the army. Mulan was helped by Mushu, a magical dragon sent by her ancestors.

One day in the snowy mountains, enemy soldiers surrounded the army. The Chinese troops were outnumbered, and their brave leader, Captain Shang, knew it was only a matter of time before they were defeated.

"There has to be a way to win," Mulan said to Mushu. Mushu held his hands over his ears as the cannons echoed through the mountains.

"Do those things have to be so loud?" he asked. That gave Mulan an idea.

"Mushu, you're brilliant!" she said.

Mulan hurried to one of the cannons and pointed it high above the heads of the enemy.

"You won't hit anything like that," her fellow soldiers said.

"Just watch," said Mulan as she fired the cannon.

A cannonball sailed over the heads of the enemies and struck the mountain behind them. The cannonball shook the mountain and the snow on top came crashing down its side in an avalanche, burying the enemy army. But Captain Shang was buried too. Mulan rode her horse over the dangerous snow until she reached Shang. She pulled him out of the snow.

"Get on," she said in a deep voice. Captain Shang leapt onto Mulan's horse and rode away as the enemy army struggled beneath the snow.

"You're the bravest man I know!" Captain Shang told Mulan.

Later, Mulan's disguise was uncovered, but that didn't stop her from saving the emperor and China before returning to her proud family!

### The End

Tick the name of the magical dragon in the story.

**MULAN**

**MUSHU**

Answer on page 69.

47

# Heads or Tails?

Play this game on your own or with a friend where you take turns to flip a coin.

**HOW TO PLAY**

Flip a coin. If it lands on 'heads' pick an action from that column. If it lands on 'tails' choose an activity to do on the page or on an extra piece of paper if you need it.

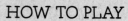

## Heads

## Tails

### CARING

Pretend to be Snow White and sing a song.

Draw a tiara for Belle.

### ADVENTUROUS

Pretend to be Rapunzel and leap into the air.

Draw an animal friend for Ariel.

### INDEPENDENT

Pretend to be Jasmine and do a twirl.

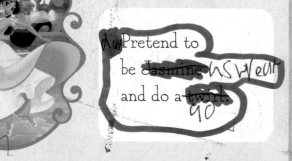

Draw a present for your friend.

*My friend's name*

........................................

........................................

48

# Explore Your WORLD

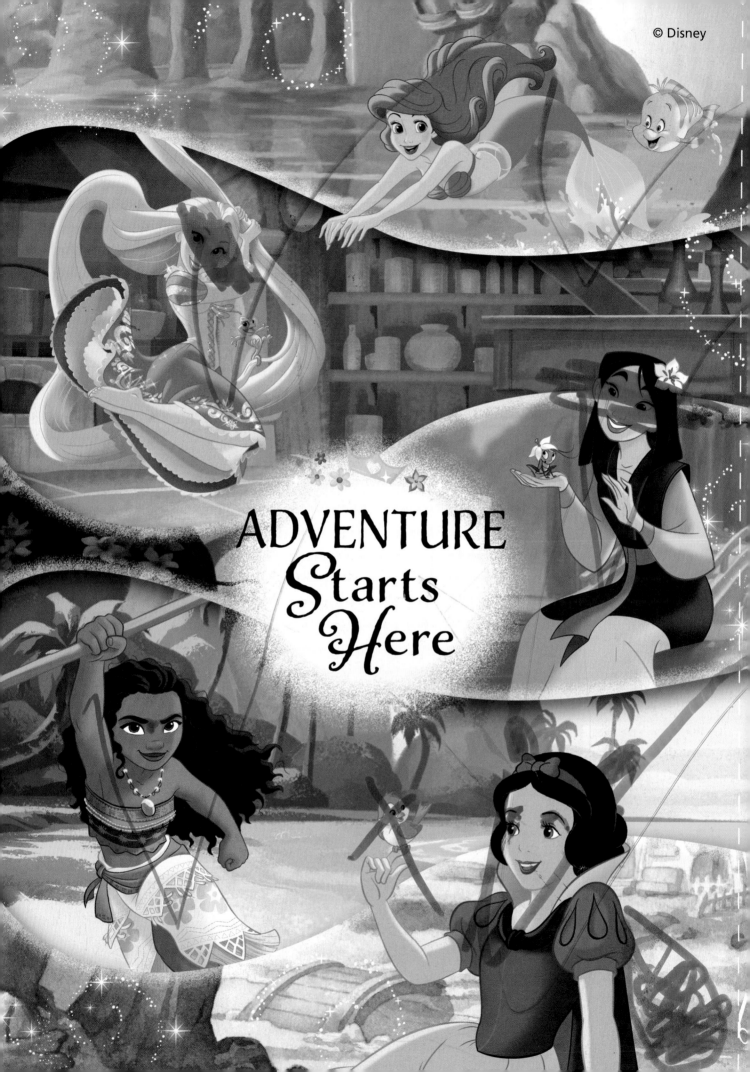

ADVENTURE
Starts
Here

# Animal Friends

**1** Colour in Moana, Ariel and Rapunzel's animal friends.

These princesses all have special animal friends who they love very much.

Moana

Rapunzel

Ariel

**2** Now draw your dream pet!

51

# Meet ... Rapunzel

★ **Rapunzel is ...**
creative, positive and fun.

❋ **Rapunzel loves ...**
painting pictures and her pet chameleon, Pascal.

✿ **Rapunzel dreams ...**
of exploring the world.

❧ **Rapunzel's story ...**
Rapunzel was kidnapped by Mother Gothel as a baby. She was brought up in a tower and locked away from the world. Her life changed forever when she met Flynn Ryder. Rapunzel escaped the tower and discovered a world of magic and love was waiting for her.

*Best day ever!*

# Swinging Around

**1** Join the dots and colour in Rapunzel.

1
2
3
4
5
20
17
6
19 18 16
15 7
14
13 8
9
12
10
11

**2** Find Pascal on this page.

53

# Up in the Tower

Read along with the story. Each time you get to a picture, say the word out loud.

RAPUNZEL    TOWER    MOTHER GOTHEL    HAIR    PASCAL    FLYNN RYDER

 lived in a tall, tall  with  .

She had no idea that  had stolen her from her

parents when she was a baby. Poor  had been

locked in the  for nearly eighteen years!

 had  that was as long as the

and it had special powers.  used 's

magic  to stay young and beautiful.

Every day,  would paint, bake and play in her with her pet chameleon, . She was happy but she was desperate to go outside.

refused. was never allowed out of her .

Until one day, climbed up the and begged him to take her outside. agreed.

Finally, it was 's chance. and were free from the and from .

It was time to discover the world!

# Rapunzel and Me

Rapunzel invites you to join in with her busy day.

**1** Tick ✔ all the activities you would like to do with Rapunzel.

Painting

Racing

Playing Guitar

Knitting

**2** Colour in Rapunzel as she tries on her tiara.

*Dressing Up*

**3** Draw pictures of your favourite activities.

# Meet ... *Aurora*

**Aurora is ...**
happy, graceful and gentle.

**Aurora loves ...**
to sing and dance with her
animal friends.

**Aurora wishes ...**
to make her friends
happy every day.

**Aurora's story ...**
Born into a royal family,
Aurora is cursed by the evil fairy
Maleficent. To keep her safe, her
father sends Aurora to live in the
forest with three good fairies. She
lives peacefully for a time, but
when she returns to the castle the
curse begins to catch up with her ...

*Everything is
so wonderful!*

# Surprise!

The good fairies have surprised Aurora with a beautiful dress and a delicious birthday cake.

1

The fairies have also hidden 5 cherry cupcakes around the room. Yum! Colour a cake when you find each one.

2

How many candles can you count on the cake?

*I count* 7 *cakes.*

Answer on page 69.

# Meet ...

# *Snow White*

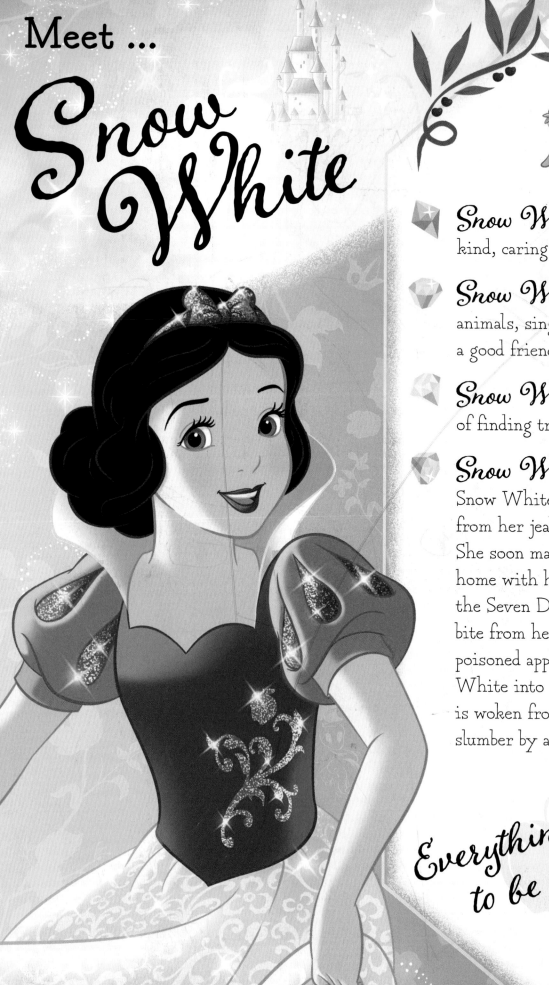

**Snow White is ...** kind, caring and thoughtful.

**Snow White loves ...** animals, singing and being a good friend.

**Snow White dreams ...** of finding true love.

**Snow White's story ...** Snow White is forced to flee from her jealous stepmother. She soon makes a happy home with her new friends, the Seven Dwarfs, but one bite from her stepmother's poisoned apple puts Snow White into a deep sleep. She is woken from her deathly slumber by a charming prince.

*Everything's going to be alright.*

# Friend or Foe?

Snow White's animal friends are waiting for her. Which path should Snow White take to reach her friends?

Watch out for the path that leads to the poisoned apple!

Answer on page 69.

# Forest Flowers

Snow White has gone into the forest to pick some flowers. Here's how to make pretty paper flowers for you!

**You will need:**

Coloured tissue paper

Scissors

Pipe cleaner

Ask a grown-up for help.

Colour in Snow White.

**1** Stack 8 squares of coloured tissue paper on top of each other. Fold the paper into zig-zags.

**2** Wind a pipe cleaner around the middle of the folded paper. Snip the ends of the paper into points with scissors.

**3** Separate the layers of tissue paper - one at a time - first on one side, then the other.

**4** Keep going until your flower takes shape.

### TIP

Instead of pipe cleaners, use a paper clip or sticky tape and make flowers without stems.

**5** Use different coloured tissue paper to make a collection!

# Meet ... Jasmine

❋ **Jasmine is ...**
stubborn, friendly and curious.

❋ **Jasmine loves ...**
her pet tiger, Rajah.

❋ **Jasmine dreams ...**
of being free and seeing the world.

❋ **Jasmine's story ...**
Although Jasmine leads a life of royal luxury with her father, the Sultan, she feels trapped and bored. When Aladdin arrives and takes her on a magic carpet ride, a whole new world opens up before her. Jasmine is ready for adventure!

*It's all so magical!*

# Swirl and Twirl

Jasmine loves to clap, twirl, jump and spin as she dances. How do you like to dance?

**1** Spot 5 differences between these pictures of Jasmine dancing.

**2**

Colour a number every time you find a difference.

     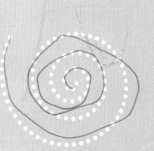 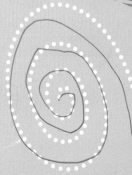

Answer on page 69.

**3**

Help Jasmine practise her spins by tracing over these spirals.

# Checkmate

Jasmine is enjoying a game of chess with Abu. Who do you want to win?

1   Look at the picture and answer 'True' or 'False' to each sentence below.

Circle your answers.

a   Jasmine is wearing a red dress.

True      False

b   Abu is standing on one leg.

True      False

2   Find this chess piece on the page.

c   Jasmine looks sad.

True      False

Answer on page 69.

# Dancing Game

Colour in Tiana and Mulan. Then, follow these princess steps to create a fun dance routine.

## How to play

1. Throw a dice onto the page.
2. Copy the move of the princess you land on.
3. Throw twice more so you have three dance moves to practise.
4. To create a new dance, throw again!

### Tiana
Curtsey up and down three times.

**2** ### Jasmine
Stand on one leg, arms out and palms facing outwards.

**3** ### Aurora
Rise up on your tiptoes and step quickly back and forth.

### Rapunzel
Legs wide, throw your arms upwards and outwards.

**5** ### Ariel
Arms swaying, skip round in a circle.

**6** ### Mulan
Freeze in a pose for three seconds.

© Disney

# Girl POWER

Colour this poster with
your favourite crayons.

# Answers

PAGE 9 *Royal Maze*

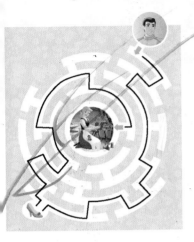

PAGE 10 *A New Friend*
. The colt has a pear.
. a   food and water

PAGE 14 *Perfect Pet*

AGE 17 *Talented Tiana*

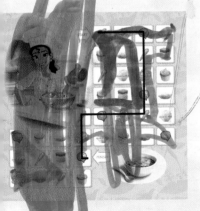

AGE 22 *Furry Intruder*
.. 6   **2.**  a, c, e and g

3.

PAGE 30 *Coconut Fun*
**1.** b   **2.** b   **3.** a and d

PAGE 31 *Moana the Hero*

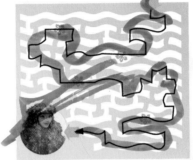

There are 4 floating flowers.

PAGE 32 *Pua Saves the Day*
**1.** b   **2.** a and c

PAGE 37 *Under the Sea*
**1.** Row 1 - c, Row 2 - a, Row 3 - b.
**2.** Book, soap dish and ice skate don't belong in the sea.

PAGE 38 *Ocean Doodles*

PAGE 45 *Fearless Mulan*
**1.** Row 1 - c, Row 2 - b, Row 3 - a.   **2.** Cri-Kee

PAGE 46 *Time for Courage*
Mushu

PAGE 53 *Swinging Around*
Pascal is hiding among the flowers at the top left.

PAGE 59 *Surprise!*
**1.**

**2.** I count 13 candles.

PAGE 61 *Friend or Foe?*

PAGE 65 *Swirl and Twirl*

PAGE 66 *Checkmate*
a. False, b. True, c. False.